Baseball

Baseball Strategies

The Top 100 Best Things That You Can Do To Improve Your Baseball Game

By Ace McCloud
Copyright © 2015

Disclaimer

The information provided in this book is designed to provide helpful information on the subjects discussed. This book is not meant to be used, nor should it be used, to diagnose or treat any medical condition. For diagnosis or treatment of any medical problem, consult your own physician. The publisher and author are not responsible for any specific health or allergy needs that may require medical supervision and are not liable for any damages or negative consequences from any treatment, action, application or preparation, to any person reading or following the information in this book. Any references included are provided for informational purposes only. Readers should be aware that any websites or links listed in this book may change.

Table of Contents

Introduction 6

Chapter 1: Baseball Nutrition 8

Chapter 2: Mental Strategies 11

Chapter 3: Improving your Baseball Swing........... 17

Chapter 4: Batting Strategies................................21

Chapter 5: Perfecting Your Pitch 23

Chapter 6: Off Season Strategies 25

Chapter 7: Fielding Positions and Strategies 28

Conclusion 36

My Other Books and Audio Books 37

DEDICATED TO THOSE WHO ARE PLAYING THE GAME OF LIFE TO

WIN

KEEP ON PUSHING AND NEVER GIVE UP!

Ace McCloud

Be sure to check out my website for all my Books and Audio books.

www.AcesEbooks.com

Introduction

With a mighty swing and a satisfying crack of the bat, the baseball flies out of the stadium to the excitement of your teammates and everyone watching! Baseball is an extremely fun and exciting game filled with strategy, intrigue and action. It can also be very complicated and difficult to master, especially as the competition increases. Being good at baseball can be a long road of blood, sweat and tears, but it is all worth it when you can perform to the best of your abilities and help your team win!

Baseball is not just about the glory; there are a lot of things involved that make a great baseball player. Baseball takes commitment over the long term and if you are doing things correctly, you will reap many positive benefits. In this book you will discover many different strategies to help you bring your baseball game to the next level. There is nothing worse than wasting your time doing things that are not going to give you the best results possible. Baseball is not just about pitching, catching, batting and running. There are many other elements to the sport that can be broken down into smaller segments that can make a huge difference in your game. From batting strategies, training strategies, motivational strategies, mental strategies and much more so that you can come to the game confident, prepared and ready for action.

This is important in all sports, but especially with baseball. You have to have strength, in order to have a powerful swing, throw the baseball accurately and be quick when running around the bases. You must also have agility, in order to catch line drives, be feared on the bases and place the bat on the ball accurately. You need to constantly be thinking about your next move and anticipating the moves of those around you. This book will help you see all the different things that you can to improve your game as a whole.

One of the biggest mistakes that any athlete can make is not fueling his or her body properly. There are so many fad diet and fitness trends on the market today that it's important to properly research your diet and training decisions so that you're treating your body like the valuable machine that it is. This means fueling it properly and it also means rewarding it (specifically your muscles) with proper nutrition and restoration that will be vital for your continued success. You won't find tips in here encouraging you to take unhealthy supplements or to try gimmicky things that are not proven to work. What you will find is an assortment of healthy eating ideas as well as strong advisements about proper stretching, strength training, mental discipline and much more.

As an extra incentive to "get your head in the game", we have a whole section on mental strategies that will help keep you focused and inspired to perform at your best every day, whether it is a game day or not. If you believe in yourself, then your team mates will believe in you. If your team mates believe in you, your coach is exponentially more likely to believe in you. If your coach believes in you, then you have a lifelong ally which you can and should depend on. There is a really special bond between a player and coach. Your coach knows exactly what you're going through, especially since he or she's probably been through similar scenarios before. This means he or she will know just how to push you and also how to support and encourage you.

We will also talk about alternative methods of peak performance so that you're relaxed, focused and full of energy before any game or practice. After reading this book you will have a variety of proven techniques that you can add to your arsenal to greatly improve your baseball game. By developing a strategy that works best for you, your baseball game is sure to improve greatly. It doesn't matter if it's your first time picking up a baseball bat or if you've been working on this game for half of your life. It all comes down to having the right strategies to bring your game to the next level. Baseball is possibly the most enjoyable sport in the world to play, especially when you are performing well and helping your team win! So let's get started with all the things that you can do to improve your baseball game!

Chapter 1: Baseball Nutrition

Just like with any physical activity, nutrition is especially important if you're going to succeed in baseball. Baseball frequently subscribes to "two-a-days"— twice a day baseball training focusing on honing and toning different parts of your body.

Baseball is equally strength and cardiovascular oriented. It requires agility, concentration and balance, in addition to speed. Obviously there's a lot of running involved, especially if your team is on the offense. However, when you're on the defense you need to be able to grab the baseball and throw it with speed and precision in order to get the hitting player out. Such entails a balanced diet and consistently strong health practices.

There are three integral parts to a successful training program. These are training, nutrition and rest. Each of these are equally important and imperative if you are going to reach your full potential as a player.

You may have heard of some of the baseball greats like Mickey Mantle and Babe Ruth. These guys didn't take very good care of their health. The fact of it is, if they had, they would have been even better. Avoid being focused on losing body fat or gaining weight mass. Instead focus on fueling your body so that it's hydrated and energized, the most powerful machine that it can be.

It's not just what you eat, it's also when you eat. For optimal results, I would recommend eating 5-6 small meals throughout the day, always at least 45 minutes before you'll be doing any serious running. This gives your body the chance to digest all the nutrients and avoid serious cramps.

If there are just a couple of tips that you follow, make sure they're the following-

Stay Hydrated- There's a simple and effective way to determine how much water you should be drinking each practice. Weigh yourself before you begin and jump back on the scale when you finish. The difference is how much fluid you have lost and needs to be replaced back into your system. Another way is to multiply your weight by .67. The answer is the number of fluid ounces of water you should be drinking daily.

There's nothing wrong with Gatorade or other Electrolyte beverages. These are a fine substitute. There are also natural alternatives out on the market in the form of tablets or gels that you can drop into water if the taste is too bland for you. Whichever way you do it, make sure that you're getting your H2O. Avoid juices as these may give you a stomach ache during exercise. At all costs avoid carbonated beverages. These may cause bloating and actually dehydrate your system. The same is true for caffeinated beverages. These cause you to lose fluid. And perhaps the most obvious, avoid alcohol during practice. Not only is it illegal and dehydrating, it slows down the body's recovery process.

To break this down even further, here are additional hydrating timeline tips for baseball players. In general, drink two cups of fluids before a practice or a game. Drink 6-8 fluid ounces every 20 minutes that you're involved in a practice or a game. You should consume 24 ounces for every pound that you lose during a practice or a game.

Fueling Strategies- It's recommended to jumpstart your metabolism within an hour of first waking up. I'm sure it's been impressed upon you before, but starting your day with a healthy breakfast can only serve you positively. Several good examples of healthy breakfasts include a bowl of high fiber cereal, whole grain toast and fruit, vegetables or a bagel with peanut butter. It's so much easier than you think to explore your supermarket and find snacks and meals that you'll look forward to and will serve your body well. It just takes a little bit of research.

Your body will tend to perform better when it is moving consistently and if it is fed a small meal or snack every four hours. This gives your body an extra boost of energy and keeps you from getting lethargic from over eating. Always eat at least an hour before practice or a game and always eat about fifteen minutes after the end of a practice or game. This is a good opportunity to snack on granola or a cereal bar, trail mix, almonds, dried fruits or a protein bar.

When it comes to lunch and dinner, make sure to include carbohydrates, since this is the food group that your body is going to burn the fastest when working out. Some good carbohydrates include bagels, bread, pasta, spaghetti, crackers, tortillas, potatoes and even fruit. You may not realize it, but fruits are an excellent source of healthy carbohydrates which are easy to burn up and give good energy.

Unlike other sports, baseball doesn't break down foods containing proteins and fats as much, so try to avoid them in large quantities. Your pre and post-game foods should specifically be lower in fats since any foods that have higher fat quantities will stay in your body longer, even causing your stomach stress or discomfort. If you need options for good protein choices, look for veal, fish, shellfish, eggs, yogurt, dried beans, or beef.

Baseball is a long game, and sometimes these games go far into the night. You'll need to plan ahead for late night snacks so that you're not gravitating towards the nearest fast food restaurant. Here are some good ideas for hearty snacks that won't give you a stomach ache- grilled chicken sandwich, ham sub, eggs and toast, fruit smoothie and almonds are great for energy.

Baseball is also a sport where you're going to need to listen to your body. You can eat a lot more because you're moving a lot more but you're going to have to time your snacks and meals effectively because they can only help or hurt you. Try different proteins, carbohydrates, fruits and veggies to see how they affect your energy levels. Remember that eating well is your first line of offense in becoming a powerful baseball player.

For some more information on the best way to eat to be in great health for your next season, check out Baseball-Nutrition by SportsMED Orthopaedic Surgery and Spine Center.

Chapter 2: Mental Strategies

There are many different types of players on a baseball team, with all sorts of different personalities. This means that everyone will react to the same situation differently. It's one thing to encourage players to be self-motivated, however it's entirely another to instill healthy aggression, effective communication and internal drive to succeed on and off the baseball field.

There is also the issue of the passive aggressive players, who need to be drawn out of their shells more so than the self-motivated players. There are many tools that coaches should have in their arsenals for situations like this. This includes real success stories, motivational speeches and anecdotes about well-known players who have overcome the odds. Sometimes visual motivation is the key for a coach, showing a picture of a championship ring or trophy.

Different types of players need to be motivated in different ways. Here's a look at a few different personalities that you may find yourself identifying with on a baseball team-

The Competitive Player- Coaches want as many of their players as possible to be competitive, to play to win. Experts refer to baseball as a failure-oriented game which can bring out negative emotions and really break down the confidence of the players involved. Baseball training puts a lot of pressure on each player to see how they react under tough situations. The drills used in practices and the plays used in games are metrics for coaches, trying to figure out how motivated a player is. One good way to tell if someone has a competitive personality is that type of person will almost always want another chance to succeed. It's okay if this drive isn't born into a person, it can be created with the right tools. These tools include dividing players into teams during practice so that they're competing against each other for a top slot. Another way to drive competition is to offer prizes, whether tangible or intangible to reward players who perform well.

The Passive Player- the passive player is at the other end of the spectrum from the competitive player. However there is a difference between a passive player and a quiet player, which is important to call out. Just because a player isn't chatty on and off the field, does not mean that they're not secretly driven. Conversely, a passive player may be chatty, but not driven at all once he is on the field. With players like this, coaches should pick drills which drive the players out of their comfort zones. Whether that's sprint drills, moving more quickly, getting dirty or practicing somewhere new and unexpected, this may drive them to perform better under pressure and develop aggression and motivation, because there is no other option. Showing these players video footage of themselves in these drills is helpful as well.

The Aggressive Player- Even more competitive than the competitive player, and sometimes too much so, is the aggressive player. This player goes full speed ahead, no matter what they're working on. Aggression is a great skill in baseball, but it needs to be properly harnessed. If it is not, the player may make mistakes or not have the ability to relax, which gets in the way of developing talent. The aggressive player requires a different motivation, learning to control his skill and play it smart on and off the field. It's a fine line because you don't want to put any restrictions on the instincts, but do ensure that this player remains not just talented on his own, but part of a team. The aggressive player requires a plan as he tends to act solely on impulses. Take the hitter for example. Tell him to only hit pitches coming from a specific area. This helps hone his impulses, because if you tell him to bat pitches coming in waist high or above, he will have to avoid low pitches that his impulses would have previously told him to chase.

The Smart Player- Even though the smart player might not have the most physical talent out of everyone on the team, he capitalizes on his knowledge of the game and his strategy. This player is absolutely vital because he can understand what the coach is thinking and stay ahead of the opposition in the game. This player needs to be motivated through brain trust, instead of physical drills and plays. The smart player can be the link between the teammates and the coach if he feels like he understands the reasoning behind training strategies. He'll look for minor tweaks that he can make in his game, by watching the opposition. You may have a shortstop who notices the hitter has hit two foul balls that have traveled right down the line of the right field. He may take two steps to his left to anticipate that this hitter may repeat this.

The Negative Player- Some players may dwell on the negative. This might be a feeling that they project on their own skills, or it might be a mindset that they unleash on the whole team, using foul language, throwing of equipment, or disruptive behavior. This player offers a challenge motivationally for the team and the coach, because there are so many negatives in baseball in general. However this attitude cannot be tolerated. The player needs to be taught that mistakes happen, that they need to be accepted and moved on from. Otherwise the whole team is impacted. If you bring a negative attitude to your team, no matter how talented you are, you'll likely end up sitting on the bench. If you're a talented player sitting on the bench and missing out on the game, your teammates will grow to resent you because they would prefer to have you out on the field. Remember that if you're having a day when you've woken up on the wrong side of the bed, to check your attitude at the door and only bring your baseball game to practice.

It's important to remember that baseball is a fail more often than you succeed sport. Even if you fail 7 out of 10 times, that is considered a great success as a hitter in baseball. This is a rarity in sports. There are not many examples where this would be considered a strong ratio. The most important thing is to believe in yourself at all times. The second largest necessity is to have a plan in mind by the time you reach the mound.

Mental Strategies

As you're walking towards the batter box, take a look at the pitcher. Is he right handed or left handed? Is he throwing from the first base side of the rubber or the third base side of the rubber? Is he throwing over the top for the other batters? What kind of arm angle is he using for the other batters? These are also answers that can help inform you in the way you should be swinging the bat in order to have greater success.

More specifically you can take a look at his style when he throws different pitches. Take a look at his fastball and the speed at which he's throwing. He may be throwing with a firm hand, or he might be faking out the pitchers by deceptively throwing with a loose grip at the last minute. His fast ball may go straight for the batter, or it might cut one direction. This will greatly impact the way that you swing your bat.

You can get an early lead on this detective work by watching all pitchers during their warm-ups. They will definitely run through each of their pitch styles to make sure that their arsenals are ready prior to the game. If you keep an even closer eye on the pitchers during their warm-up, you may learn what signals they give the catchers for each pitch.

It can only help to know the other players on opposing teams. Be it mutual friends or general knowledge of their personality and playing style, you'll get to know their styles in advance of playing them so that you can strategize ways to challenge their weak spots.

If the pitcher is throwing for strikes, and doing so successfully, he will usually try to throw them to his dominant side. This means he'll throw inside to those who are right handed and outside to those who are left handed, if the pitcher is right handed. He will also be sure to throw any sinkers to his glove side. The premise of a sinker pitch is that the baseball's movement will encourage the hitter to accidentally hit a grounder that will be easy for infielders to pick up. These pitchers like to complement their sinker shots with slider shots. This is a pitch that will maximize the glove side of home plate. The pitchers goal here is to get you to mistake where you're seeing the ball. This can completely change your swing velocity. Make sure that you engage your mental toughness when you're hitting against a pitcher that loves sinker balls. His thought process is that you will get yourself out if you hit the ball in play. He wants those grounders. If you're aware of this in advance, you can avoid this trick.

The next way to strategize is to look at all of the situations in the game currently. Take a look at the bases and where your opponents are. Maybe there is a player on first and second base. Then you can bunt the ball or try to hit it out of the park. Since baseball is a team sport, you can't be selfish when batting because you'll end up striking out, and not assisting in the advancement of those already on bases. You need to take the positions of everyone on the field into account. This goes back to taking your time. This isn't a timed sport. Some have joked that it's the longest game in sport out there. So take a deep breath, take a look around and make your strategic decisions wisely.

Improving Your Confidence

Confidence is a great way to improve the way you play baseball. Some ways you can improve your confidence include:

80/20 Rule. Knowing how to use the 80/20 rule to your advantage is an important, core habit that you should learn before trying out any of the next couple of habits. Basically, this rule suggests that you should focus on the most important 20% of what you're working on to increase your peak results by 80%. This is a powerful technique that can help you in all areas of life, not just with self-confidence, so it is important to know what 20% of the task to focus the majority of your attention on.

Visualization. Visualization is another core habit that is a very powerful and useful technique. When you practice visualization, your chances of achieving a goal that you have been thinking and visualizing about can increase dramatically. By visualizing yourself having already achieved your goal, you can use the feel-good vibes to increase your chances of actually accomplishing it. Be as specific as you can in your visualizations—think about how you'll feel, what you'll look like, what you'll touch, what you'll smell, etc. It's also a good idea to visualize yourself accomplishing all the steps that will lead up to your goal, and using a far away "camera angle" can increase the effectiveness of visualization.

Think About Your Good Qualities. By focusing on the qualities about yourself that are good, you can help yourself gain a high level of self-confidence. For example, if you're about to give an oral report and you're nervous, but you know that you're a very organized person, focus on that and your chances of doing great can be bigger.

Reflect on Positive Experiences. Many people with low self-esteem tend to wallow on negative past experiences. By thinking about times when you felt you're greatest, you can use those examples to push forward into the future. For example, think about a time when you made a great hit or baseball play. Remember how good it felt and what you did. Your chances of feeling more confident in the moment can increase by doing this. It's also a good idea to make a journal and record of all your favorite positive experiences that you have had throughout your life. You can include pictures, awards, events, friends, anything else that makes you happy. Then, be sure and read through this journal a couple of times a week to keep your spirits high.

"Stop" Negative Thoughts. Learn how to become more aware of when you start thinking negatively and then say "stop," either out loud or internally. Many therapists use this technique and you can do it yourself, anywhere. This can prevent you from getting too wrapped up in negative emotions that can bring down your self-confidence. To learn some awesome and easy do-it-yourself techniques on how to stop thinking negatively, I invite you to check out this YouTube video by Nathaniel Solace: <u>Negative Thoughts: How to Stop Negative Thoughts, Fear, Stress & Self Doubt</u>.

Be Thankful. Be thankful for the things that you *do* have as opposed to thinking about the things that you *don't* have. When you think about things that you want, your mind tends to start focusing on your weaknesses that prevent you from having those things. By being thankful, you can live more positively and you can feel it more in your confidence. Try and list thirty things that you are thankful for each day.

Practice Good Posture. When you slouch or slump over, you are essentially sending a message to other people that you have low self-confidence. In turn, that could deter people from approaching you and you may start to feel less confident in being social. When you practice good posture, such as standing tall and strong, it shows that you are proud of yourself and it may make you more approachable. When you stand tall, it helps you feel important internally. Be sure to practice making eye contact and keeping your head up, too. For a good video on how to practice good posture, check out this helpful YouTube video by Posture Confidence, <u>How To Get Good Posture</u>.

Dress Well. The way you dress often says a lot about you and can influence how you feel about yourself. By dressing well, you can make yourself look even better than you already are and you can feel more empowered. Although it may feel like others judge you by the way you dress, the person who judges you the most tends to be yourself. That being said, you don't have to dress up in a suit or tie every day. Just try to avoid wearing dirty, wrinkled, ripped, or old clothing. Look presentable and well groomed.

Be Heard. People who have low levels of self-confidence tend to stay quiet when they are in large groups. This usually happens out of a fear of being judged. However, it is important to remember that not everybody is as judging as you think! Even by just speaking up once or twice every time you're around people, you can help yourself get better at public speaking, which can really help you become more confident. For some very helpful tips on improving your public speaking skills, check out the informative YouTube video called <u>How To Speak Up Without Freaking Out</u>, posted by Dice News. It's aimed toward public speaking at work but you can always apply the principles to other situations.

Make Contributions. Making contributions to other people and projects can be a great way to become more confident. You could donate old clothes, volunteer your time, give some food, mentor a child, or anything else you can think of. When you lend your service to others, it generally helps you feel better about yourself, knowing that you helped out somebody who is going through a rough time.

Get to Know Yourself. Knowing yourself and what you like is a major way to become more confident. When you know yourself, what you want, what you like, where you want to be, etc, you can have a better sense of control over your life. A good way to get to know yourself better is to engage in some alone time. A good idea may be to start a journal, where you can pour out your deepest thoughts.

Live By Your Values. Most people have core values, such as family, religion, morales, etc. Your values serve as another foundation of how you make decisions in life. Live by your values and make the decisions in the best light that reflects your values. This can help you become more fulfilled and confident in the long-run. For a better idea of core values and some examples, check out the informative YouTube video called What Are Personal Core Values, posted by values test quiz.

Set and Achieve Small Goals. By setting and achieving small goals, you can build your confidence up to the point where you feel ready and able to take on bigger and more long-term goals. You can even make it easier to accomplish a long-term goal by breaking it down into short-term goals. A great idea is to always start your goal off with the phrase: "I will easily..."

Meditate. Meditation is a powerful way to help yourself engage in your thoughts and learn how to control them. Meditation is easy and you can do it anywhere, as long as you are comfortable with what you're wearing and you have a peaceful, quiet place to do it. It can be very refreshing for your mind and it can really help you harness your confidence. Check out two great YouTube meditations– Meditation Music Amazing Brain Sound Dopamin Booster Pineal Gland, posted by awakenings channel; and Best Ever Gong Meditation May 20th 2013, posted by Gongster.

Forgiveness. Being able to forgive is critical in order for you to be able to focus on more important things than the bad memories and trauma of the past. Although forgiveness can be extremely difficult, it can be one of the most important things you do for your overall mental wellbeing. For advanced knowledge on how to forgive, check out my book: Forgiveness.

Be Humble. Avoid bragging and other ego-inflating activities. Be humble and modest and you can feel more confident. When you act this way, your confidence can naturally shine through you and you won't have to put so much effort into trying to impress others.

Chapter 3: Improving your Baseball Swing

There are many components to improving your baseball skills. The first and perhaps the most important thing that you can improve upon is your swing. Let's break down some strategies that can improve your swing. As an added visual, ProSwingNY has a great YouTube video with the 7 Steps to a Perfect Baseball Swing. Let's cover the five phases for a perfect swing.

The first thing to keep in mind is rhythm. A good rhythm is what will help you relax and ensure that you're ready to swing at the right time. When you have a good rhythm going, you can improve the timing of your reactions and ultimately make contact with the baseball much more frequently.

The mantra in your head should be, "relax and be ready to explode." When you watch a tennis player who is returning his or her serve or you see a basketball player going in for a score, the movement and mindset is the same. Take a deep breath and channel your power into your swing. Practice this by going through the motion and timing your breathing accordingly. Breathe in as you pull your bat back over your shoulder and exhale as you follow through. Practice this over and over again until it feels like second nature to you. You never want to be too tense or too rigid, you want to be nice and relaxed.

Find your stance. Make sure that your feet are about a hip width apart and that your weight is evenly distributed. You should be able to bounce from foot to foot without bouncing up and down too much. Your knees should be bent and your rear end should stick out slightly behind you. This small amount of movement in your legs keeps you relaxed and ensures that you remain in control. Your rhythm helps your speed and your speed helps you make adjustments much more quickly.

Remember that your physical approach is not going to be nearly as successful if you don't have a strategy in mind. This is what is going to separate the great hitters, the ones that make it in the hall of fame, from the good ones. When you are prepared with a great strategy, you'll be more confident at practice and perform better at your games. These strategies will help to motivate you and encourage you to become more of a leader on your team.

The second stage for improving your swing revolves around your load. In order to have a powerful swing, you need to load up, which provides a coiled tension. This is what provides the explosive power in your swing. Loading is basically when you lift your front leg and step slightly back, putting pressure on your back leg, allowing you to explode forward powerfully a few seconds later. Check out this great video from BaseballMastery.com called load to launch, to see this in full detail. There are various different ways to load up to hit the baseball, so be sure to take your time, experiment and find out which way works best for you. Some people like to step back further, some hit better with a smaller step back, some have more pronounced loads and some like to step back raising their lead leg higher. Nothing is worse than doing something over and over again for years at a time that is not the ideal way for you to do it! Put in the time and effort and determine the best way of loading up that gives the best results for you.

We've just discussed rhythm, and the load relies on successful timing as well. The load is a great timing device. It continues your rhythm. There are a couple of different ways that you can load up. You can use a leg kick. You can use a toe tap. You can use a normal stride or just pick up your heel. This small movement helps you make your next move as impactful as possible.

Let's take a more intensive look at the load. Your starting point has your weight distributed evenly, in between your front leg and your back leg. As far as timing goes, when the pitcher begins to lift his leg, you want to begin shifting your weight on to your back foot. Adjust your weight distribution from 50/50 to 60/40. Once you have the hang of it, you can build on the energy in your load by pulling 100% of your weight into your back leg, cocking your hip and leaning everything you have into the baseball. Make sure that you don't let the knee that's in back go outside of your back foot. This can cause injury. Your knee needs to stay inside of your foot so that your balance is taken advantage of and you're in the most athletic pose possible.

Now let's talk about the hands. When you push the weight back in your legs, you'll find that your hands also begin to load and they move back in the direction of the catcher. This means your hands will be their strongest and most enabled to move in the direction of the baseball. It's the same movement you would make if you were about to punch someone in the face.

There's an interesting relationship between weight and the amount of load that you will be able to propel forward. With less weight you will have less power to rocket forward. However, with more weight, you will most likely have more strength to take advantage of. Regardless, make sure that your body has the straightest alignment possible in the direction of the pitcher. Don't turn your back away from the ball. This can have a negative effect on your swing. Your swing will become more rotational, which means it will be in and out of the strike zone. The bottom line is that your success at hitting the ball won't be nearly as consistent if you turn your back away from the ball.

Part three of a successful swing is the separation stage. This is where you want to feel the most powerful right before hitting the ball. At this stage you want to separate the mechanics of your hands' movements from the stride of your feet. This separation causes torque. The torque means that your launch position is balanced and that your position is strong. The process of separation begins as your load completes, and finishes when your front foot first hits the ground. This may feel like the phase of the swing when your brain is most engaged, because it's the part of the swing when the ball first leaves the pitcher's hand.

Your hands should be in a position of strength, around the height of your shoulders. Use your shoulder muscles and outside oblique muscles so that your body is pulling away from you in the opposite direction. The top priority here is to move slowly and with control. To practice this, try walking around while balancing a book on your head. You may wonder why you want to move with such precision during this phase. It's so that you have your eye trained on the ball and know exactly where it's going. The more you can separate, the more precision and power you will have when your bat finally makes contact with the ball.

Your weight distribution in this phase should very similar to when you're in the load phase, about 60% should be placed on your back foot. Ensure that the toe of your front foot is softly placed in the dirt and pop your heel up in the air. Your feet should be in line and your body should be aligned with the pitcher. Your stride should be neither closed nor open at this point in the swing.

It's important to reiterate that your hands are still back. They're roughly the height of your shoulder behind you. If you need a precise angle, your bat should be around 45 degrees.

As discussed earlier, this is an intense time when you need to keep eye contact. As soon as the ball leaves the pitcher's hands, the pressure is on and you need to be orchestrating a strategy for your next move.

If you're struggling with the logistics of this phase, don't spend too much time worrying about it. The separation is the one of the most difficult to master and it's tough to replicate over and over again. However, just because it's hard does not mean that you shouldn't practice day in and day out until you feel comfortable.

Stage four is referred to as the weight shift. This initiates more of the torque action that we've discussed and helps to propel your hands into the strike zone.

After you complete your separation, you'll be in your launch position. Allow your heel to make contact with the ground beneath you. You'll notice that your back knee will gain ground on your front knee as it rotates. You want to make sure that you're moving your weight so that it starts a path towards the baseball in a very straight line. You've already changed your focus towards the ball in stage three, now you is when begin your movement towards the ball and shift the weight of your entire body. When you finish the separation step, your toe will be on the ground but your foot will be in the air. Once your front heel touches the ground, everything moves into motion for this stage.

To help with this move, drive your back hip directly into the home plate. It may feel like a very small movement but you're capitalizing on gravity to stay on top of the baseball which allows you to swing downhill. If you practice this technique, you exponentially improve your chances of hitting the baseball. You want to feel like the front side of you is pushing this motion back. Once you initiate your swing, your leg will have maximum power. This action increases the tension that causes a rotation around your head.

Your hands are going to be a direct extension of what's going on with your base, that's your foundation. If you have strength in the drive of your leg, you've already set yourself up for success because you have a proper bat path. You're also going to get your bat in the hitting zone much faster and you'll ultimately hit the baseball with much more authority.

The bottom line on this stage is all about the shift in weight and ensuring that your foundation is sturdy and strong. Be engaged in this moment because any lapses in attention can cause mid-swing adjustments that will have you missing tricky pitches.

The final stage of a successful swing is the follow through. You've already shifted your weight towards the ball as you're leaning to hit it. Bring the bat up and over your body in a diagonal motion. Don't bend your arms into your body but rather move them in a semi-circular rotation in front of your body and then up over your shoulder. Your rear toe will drag towards your front foot as you hit the ball.

Chapter 4: Batting Strategies

Now that we've broken down the components of a successful swing, let's discuss other helpful hitting strategies. The first is to look away and adjust to pitches that are flying inside. Pitchers try to keep the ball away from you. So it makes the most sense to keep your eye on the most outside edge of the plate. If you set yourself up for inside pitches, you'll have a much harder time adjusting for outside pitches than if you expect that either may be coming your way. If the pitcher throws a fastball, you may need to adjust up to 15-17 inches. If you're looking for a good drill to build up your bat speed, check out Dead Red Hitting TV's "Baseball Swing Hitting Resistance Drill to Build Bat Speed." Here are the top five strategies for batters:

1. Aim to look down the center of the plate. This is a distinctive strategy because you avoid a cluttered mindset that isn't sure where the ball is heading. You are also looking for the pitch that you can hit the hardest and get you the furthest around the bases.

2. Look for velocity. Cutters, sliders and fastballs all have similar velocities. If you're looking for this, you'll be able to style your swing direction and speed effectively. This prevents what is referred to as "being in between on pitches". Almost half of each player's hitting approach is specific to the fastball. The other half is totally dependent on speed. Your body may move too slowly on the fastball. Your body may also move too quickly for the speed so that no pitch is possible to hit.

3. Once you have your strategy in place you need to stick with it. You can change and finesse it over time as you learn the game, but you need to be committed to it 100%. Having no strategy is much worse than the worst of strategies.

4. Take your value one step further by becoming a utility player. We'll discuss the other roles on a baseball team later in this guide, but right now let's focus on the utility player, because he can fulfill so many roles on a team. The utility player has taken the time to learn each position, is useful in practice and is useful in offense. Many players in Major League Baseball will try and add on years to their careers by training to become a utility player. It makes them much harder to let go when they learn new skills, because they already know the team so well. There are many players who begin as sharp basemen, but then aren't so fast on their feet after a couple of years. However, they still may be able to hit the baseball out of the park so they can become designated as a hitter in their later playing days. Coaches and managers love these players because they make their jobs much easier. They don't need to add players to the roster or deal with new contracts and agreements.

5. We've discussed the importance of a mental strategy, and this can best be summarized as, 'keep your head in the game.' It's a cliché that is overused in many senses, but here it's extremely applicable. Looking for inspiration? Be sure to watch this YouTube video by Matt Morse: Evan Longoria E:60- The Best 10 Minutes in the Mental Game of Baseball. The mental game is half of the overall game. You need to keep your psychological senses sharp. Even though this won't necessarily make your hand and eye coordination better or speed up your swing, the results are still quantifiable.

   Chuck Knoblauch is a great example. He's the second baseman for the New York Yankees and recently discovered the "yips", as baseball fans and players refer to them. If you haven't heard of the yips, it's common across many sports. It's basically when you lose your capacity to effectively play your sport or game. With Knoblauch being a second baseman, it was very important for him to know how to throw to first base. However, due to his yips, he lost his ability to do this. In order to make him indispensable, he had to learn different positions. He was lucky he was able to do this. Steve Blass is another MLB player who has been affected by the yips. He ended up leaving the sport because he couldn't adapt to another position.

When you keep your head in the game and take the psychological strategy seriously, you are an asset to your team. This makes you a "smart player". Where large, strong, unintelligent players used to pervade the sport of baseball, they have now been replaced with those who put more emphasis on the thinking process.

Chapter 5: Perfecting Your Pitch

The important strategy here is the grip. Howcast has a great YouTube video, 9 Pitching Grips that you can watch. You want a very strong grip. A straight throw ideal grip is referred to as a 4-seam grip. You achieve this when you take your index finger and your middle finger of your throwing hand and place them perpendicular to the horseshoe that's shown on the seams of your baseball. When you successfully master this grip, your fingers are poised to utilize the seams. They can pull down and increase your rotation backwards. This also causes the ball to rotate straight and rotate true. If you alter this and place your fingers parallel instead of perpendicular, then your ball is going to frequently spin left or right, because it's catching the wind resistance.

Once you feel the ball, you're going to hold it differently every time. You want to work on feeling the ball and really becoming comfortable with it. A good practice technique is to grab the ball different ways and quickly shift it to a four seam grip. Get the feel of making this adjustment no matter how you hold the ball. It's way easier than you may think. Why you may ask? Because no matter how you've grabbed the ball, you only have to turn it a quarter turn to end up with a 4-seam grip. It just takes practice.

In order to become a successful pitcher, you should become adept at throwing fastballs, curveballs, sinkers, sliders and knuckleballs. Videojug has a great series of videos demonstrating the right way to throw each of these pitches. You can watch them to learn How To Throw A Curveball In Baseball or just visit Videojug.com.

Fastballs

Step 1- get a grip. Place your index finger and middle finger about an inch apart. Cover the seams. If you cover the seams with your fingertips, it will impact your velocity. Keep step 1 hidden in your glove so that the batter can't see. Keep your foot on the rubber and take a small step back to begin your windup (step 2). Bring your pitching hand up to your hand and pivot your foot so that it's flush right up against the rubber underneath you. Now for the delivery. Focus your eyes, lift your knee, and rotate your hip. Bring your stride leg down and remove the ball from your glove. Swing your pitching arm upward. The elbow of your throwing arm should move above your shoulder as you continue to rotate your hips. Then you release the ball. Your hand should be in front of your body and your fingers should stay on top of the ball. Extend your pitching arm down. Make sure that your front leg is bent slightly and keep your foot as close to home plate as you can. The last step is your follow through. You release the ball and stiffen your front leg. Your body is making a 90 degree angle. Now your back leg can swing around and you end up in a fielding position.

Next up is the curveball. Your grip has your thumb along the seam of the baseball and your middle finger on the opposite side. Place your index finger next to your middle finger. This helps you keep control. Now take a small step backwards to begin your windup. Bring your pitching hand and your glove up to your head. Now rotate your hips and bend your other knee. This ensures maximum power and maximum balance. Lower your stride leg and start to take the ball out of your glove. Swing your pitching arm upwards and reach with your front shoulder towards home late. Check your throwing elbow. Is it above your shoulder? It should be. Turn the palm of your hand to face towards your ear as it passes your head. This movement is what makes a curveball, a curveball. Now snap your wrist towards home plate.

The knuckleball is a bit of a mystery pitch. It may go left, it may go right. To master it, begin with your grip. You want to push it in the direction of home plate with minimal rotation. Dig your ring, index and middle fingers right underneath the seams on the baseball. Again, no rotation is key here. If you push and don't rotate, the knuckleball will perform much better. Keep your wrist stiff and push with your fingers. You're also pushing your body forward so that it's at a 90 degree angle.

A slider is similar to a fastball in the way that it's thrown, but once it's in flight, it tends to veer towards the side. Many batters mistake sliders for fastballs so it's much harder to detect! Similar to a fastball, grip the baseball with your middle finger and index finger on the widest seams. Tuck your thumb under the ball. The difference is in the delivery. Keep your wrist loose and in front of your body. Your arm reaches out and then down as it releases the ball.

Finally you have the sinker pitch. Its name is significant because it's a fastball pitch that has substantial downward movement. It's frequently used when pitchers are trying for ground balls. Grip the ball on the two seams and extend your arm like you would a fastball. When it comes to delivery, slacken and your wrist and face it downward so that your hand is covering the ground. As with any sneaky pitch, make sure the ball is hidden from the batter's view until the very last minute.

To see how these baseball pitches work visit this video by Pitching Academy: Teaching How to Throw Different Baseball Pitches.

Chapter 6: Off Season Strategies

The off season can be just as important to how well you play as the on season. You need to take this time to get better at the sport and to keep your body conditioned to play again. While it is possible to take it a little easier on the off season, you should be taking some time to work on getting good sleep, keeping up your nutrition, and fixing any injuries or other issues which occurred. Here are some of the strategies you can try to keep on the top of your game, even on the off season.

Off Season Strategies for Pitchers

Charlie Green, a well-known baseball coach says that "pitchers are made during the off-season". This is a wise statement. It's important to remember that the off-season is just as important to your growth as a player as regular season practices and games. You may think, "I just had a great season! I deserve a rest." Well, that's not entirely true. Your muscles and your body deserve rehabilitation given the stress that you may have put on them. However, unless your body was in poor condition at the beginning of the season, it should not be so beat up that you need to take an extensive rest in the off-season. Pitching is a strenuous activity, but it's also one that builds up your stamina and strength when you do it repeatedly, making it easier over time. Think about the total amount of time that a pitcher is actually in action. A pitch is a two second (maximum) explosive movement. If a pitcher is pitching 50 times pre-game in the bullpen and pitching 100 times in a regular game, the pitcher has exerted himself around five minutes. Isn't it crazy how little time that breaks down to? That's not in any way to denote the importance of the pitchers job or the effort that goes into his movements. Instead, remember to focus on specific muscles and rehabilitate, rather than diving into an off-season of lazy mornings and unhealthy food. You do that, and you're right back where you started when the season begins.

So where should pitchers begin? They first need to take a look back at the season that has just finished. What worked well? What didn't work so well? There may be a game that is plaguing you and you can't get out of your head. You can't go back and change time. However you can move forward and make changes that will benefit you in the future. So make a list of things that you think you can improve upon moving forward. This list should include your ERA, your hits per inning and your strikeout to walk ratio.

You can take this one step further and have video analysis done by an expert. I strongly recommend doing this so that the aspects of the game that you can improve upon are right in front of you and can't be avoided. You'll be able to take a very specific look at your mechanical faults. These may be greatly impacting your velocity. They may also be hurting the muscles in your arm in the long term and need to be adjusted now. You need to be your own toughest critic when it comes to improvement. Your teammates, peers and coach will give you input, but it will always have a filter of a different agenda on it. When you're able to give yourself honest and helpful feedback, you've already done yourself a huge service.

Another good idea is to have an assessment done on your strength and flexibility. These can be done by a physical therapist or a certified trainer. Make sure that they have a Paul Check Certification, an ACSM, or an NASM. These are the certifications that guarantee they'll take a look at every part of your strength and flexibility. They'll be able to give you the most comprehensive analysis as to where your body stands currently and forecast any injuries that you may sustain if you continue with your current training program.

After that, the responsibility is yours to create a conditioning program for yourself. You need to develop a comprehensive schedule for all of your workouts. You want to improve your mechanics and your general pitching skills as well. You should aim to improve all types of pitches. There is no pitcher out there who couldn't work on his velocity. 5 miles per hour can make a huge difference. The same thing goes for mechanical adjustments. You're lying to yourself if you don't think that there are not at least four-five things that you could improve upon. This is why the video analysis is so helpful, you can pinpoint the elements of your game that can be improved so that your off-season training plan is perfectly finessed.

Because pitching is an activity dominated by one arm, there are a lot of imbalances that are created through the duration of a long season. This is why a strength and flexibility assessment is helpful. Make sure that this assessment includes helpful information on what areas of your body are in need of extra strengthening. The physical therapist or trainer can also alert you to any injuries that you may not be aware of. They can give you helpful advice on how to adjust your game to lessen any discomfort with these injuries. Remember that reducing the risk of these can loop right back to adjusting the mechanics of your game, something else that the physical therapist or trainer can help you with. These types of comprehensive assessments should cost around $100-$150 and you can find them at all sports medicine clinics. When you leave, the physical therapist or trainer can give you corrective exercises. These will help any imbalances, any deficits that you show in strength and any issues in flexibility which will help your overall game.

When in the off-season, you should apply the 80/20 rule. This means that 80% of your best results are going to happen from 20% of your activities. That's why it's so important that pitchers properly invest their time instead of wasting it on activities that may not have any bearing on their game improvement. If you're confused as to what these activities should be, they may be more confusing than you initially think. Don't spend too much time on towel drills. Instead focus on the specific mechanical issues that your video analysis shows you. Don't spend too much time on weight training. Focus on stabilization exercises. These include plyometrics for the lower body and medicine ball for the upper body. Don't focus on long toss, focus on mound pitching.

More Off Season Strategies

No matter what position you play, you will be able to benefit from some off season strategies. The first thing that you should do is get enough sleep in each day. When you are playing the game, your sleep schedule may get all messed up with the planes, busses, cars, and hotel stays. Figure out a way to get a more consistent sleep schedule to get the body some rest before the season starts again. Aim for 8 hours or more of sleep each night.

Keep your eating diet clean. Even in the off season you should be avoiding processed and fast food. These might taste good, but they are going to be hard on your body and you don't want to get your butt kicked when you go back for training.

Next, concentrate on hydration. When you are not out in the sun or running around, it is easy to forget that you are thirsty and need to be kept hydrated. Take the time to drink plenty because your muscles will still need the hydration to be strong until season starts again.

While you are on the off season, take the time to clean up some of the lingering or past injuries that you have. These might be slowing down your game and it will be easier to harm them without proper care. Go through a thorough assessment with a doctor or a physical trainer to see where injuries might be present, especially if you have been injured recently. They can help you to get on the training path to heal the injury and prevent another from occurring.

Getting a new foundation ready and going for the next season is important for your offseason training. You cannot afford to take the whole season off if you want to be better than the rest. You should have some sort of training procedure in place during the off season that will help you to get the edge that you want and perform your very best when the season begins again. So be sure that you have a regular cardio and strength training routine in place. It's also a great idea to hit the batting cages as often as possible.

Chapter 7: Fielding Positions and Strategies

There are many different positions on a baseball team and it's important for you to find the position that works the best for your skillset.

Most of the roles on a baseball team are defensive first and foremost. When players move over to the offensive side, it's because it is their turn at bat to be a hitter.

There are always nine players on the field. Their combined goal is get players on the other team out, and to stop the hitting team from scoring any runs. The nine positions are- catcher, pitcher, first base, second base, third base, right field, left field, centerfield and shortstop.

Unlike many other sports, the location of seven of these nine players is pretty arbitrary. The only two positions that have distinct areas that they're supposed to remain in are the catcher and the pitcher. However the other seven positions' name and areas have become standardized over the years, shifting only slightly depending on the current scenario in the game or the style of the pitcher's technique.

Defensive baseball positions can be separated into three different categories. These are infielders, outfielders and battery.

First up, the batter. The two players in the batter's box are the catcher and the pitcher. The pitcher's definitive spot will probably make the most sense. He hangs out solely on the center of the field referred to as the "pitching mound". He throws the ball towards home plate, in hopes that the catcher will catch it and that the batter will bat unsuccessfully. Any play in baseball will always start with a pitcher.

The success of a play begins with the pitcher's ability to make the batter miss the baseball coming towards him. Pitchers try and make the batters miss in two different ways, by throwing strikes and by throwing the ball where they think that batters won't be able to hit them. The difference between these is that a strike is a pitch that a batter could have hit but missed. Here is a YouTube video by NASOreferee showing the Baseball Strike Zone to help you understand how strikes work. Pitchers often have a signature style with a certain type of pitch that they're especially good at. A popular type of successful pitcher is very good at fast balls, where they try and frighten the batter. Another popular type of pitcher is one great at throwing curve balls, or sliders. Both types of pitches cause the batter to swing at the ball in the wrong place. This is one sport where the best defense is a good offense.

The catcher sits just behind the home plate. As you may guess by the name, his main goal is to catch the baseball if the batter strikes out, or if he doesn't swing at the ball. The catcher remains in a squatting position with the glove where the pitcher is directing his pitch. It's basically a target for the pitcher. You may have seen catchers during games communicating odd signals with their hands to the pitchers. This is their way of calling what type of pitch they'd recommend based on the location, strategy and grip of the hitter. These are things that the close proximity of the catcher help the pitcher out with.

Next up, we have the baseball infielders. There are four players that make up the infield on a baseball team. They are the first baseman, the second baseman, the third baseman and the shortstop. Depending on the situation, all of these players shift their positions frequently. In general, their names are pretty indicative of the areas that they cover, respectively. The first baseman is stationed right inside the first base and then a few feet back. He is responsible for covering the first base. The same is true for second baseman and third baseman with their respective bases. Shortstop also helps cover second base, if the ball falls in his territory. Here are specific strategies for all of these positions:

First Base-

- Hold runners on first base by keeping both feet in proper position. You can have your foot on the chalk line, but don't step outside of it.

- Tag players out efficiently by reaching your glove directly out to the front of the bag where he will come sliding into base. Don't tag the runner up high, that's a common mistake.

- Try to get two shuffles from first base towards second base once the pitcher has thrown the ground. You want to cover as much ground as possible. Always be in your ready position.

- Left handed players do well at first base because they have an easier time throwing to second base.

- Use your upper body. Use your core to spin you around should you need to take off after a grounder or pitch in a direction that you're not facing.

Second Base-

- When you're on second base, the likelihood that you'll need to manage double plays is much higher. There are three different types of feeds that you can use- underhand flip, backhand toss and overhand toss.

- Communicate with your shortstop. Ask him where he likes to receive the toss. This will make the toss that much smoother.

- Work smarter, not faster. Don't be too quick to assist the shortstop. He has to turn the ball. You just need to get him the baseball.

- Be prepared to receive throws not only from first base, but also from the catcher. Keep your eyes trained on both and your head in the game.

- Switch up your technique so that the runner doesn't know which way you're heading. You want to exhaust him running so that it's easier to tag him out.

Third Base-

- Third basemen often have to contend with grounders and bare hand play. Do not attempt bare hand play unless the ball is rolling slowly or has completely stopped.

- If you're running towards a grounder, open your hand as wide as you possibly can. Right before you're about to catch it, relax your hand. This small adjustment gives you a better chance of catching it.

- Look out for topspin missiles at third. If you foresee a tough topspin coming in, step back and open your stance so that you're covering more ground.

- You're the line of defense between tagging the player out and allowing the ball into the outfield, an area which doesn't have as great coverage behind third base. Be fully aware of this and ready to run in any direction to scoop up the ball.

- Practice powerful throws to first base during practice, as this will be one of the most important skills of third baseman can have.

Shortstop--

- Stay low—any time that you are approaching the ball, try to stay low. This is going to make it easier for you to see the hops that the baseball is taking-something that is difficult to do when you are standing up higher. Being low is also a more athletic position. You will find that coming up to catch the ball is easier than trying to drop down to get to it.

- Small strides—as you are going after the ball, take smaller strides. This makes it easier to change the direction you want to go as well as speed up or slow down. If you take longer strides, your foot is going to be in the air longer, slowing down your process. Small and quick strides can help to keep you moving.

- Glove position—it is often recommended that you field the ball to the left side. This makes it feel more natural to your body since the shoulder is there. Choosing to go from the middle forces the body to reach out in front. It can free up the glove hand in order to let it work more freely.

- Foot positioning—keep the left foot just a bit behind the right foot. This can make the glove hand on the left work easier and get more of a throw in the arm.

- Making the throw— this is one of the most important parts because you want to get the ball to the right place. There are two options for this part:

  o Take the right foot and move it in front of the left foot. This allows the momentum to go forward for you rather than going away a bit. With this process you will need to take a mini shuffle or hop, whichever you feel more comfortable with, to make the throw. Here is a great YouTube video by TouchEmAllBaseball called Infield Throwing Mechanics.

  o Next, take the right foot and then let it swing around so that the right one will shuffle into the left foot. Do this at least one extra time to direct the momentum in the right direction to first base.

Left Fielder

- Learn to guess—the more that you play baseball the easier it is to guess where the ball is going. When you can take a guess at where the ball is going by the type of hitter and their stance, it makes it more likely you will catch the ball.

- Be prepared—when you are on left field, you will be throwing to the third baseman primarily, so this is your cutoff player. Once you catch the ball, throw the ball immediately without delay.

- Listen to players—instead of looking around to figure out where to throw the ball, listen to your teammates. When you hear someone asking for the ball, you will be able to just turn around and get it to them without having to flail around hoping to do it right.

- Always be ready—just because you are further back than some of the other players does not mean that your job is not important. There are quite a few batters who will be able to hit hard and will send the ball your way.

- Use the cutoff player—you are the back support for third base, make sure that you are paying attention to help them out. If the ball goes past them or they miss, you are the second line of defense that needs to be there to get the person out.

Center Fielder

- Right position—when the batter comes up, you should be positioned depending on how they hit. If they are a power hitter you should be further back but for a smaller batter, come a little closer. The play will also matter; a big play should entice you to move back a little bit.

- Watch threats to stealing—a runner who is on first is going to try and steal second if possible. It is your responsibility to prevent this or at least prevent them from getting any further. If there happens to be a throw down which gets by the shortstop or second baseman, you must get the ball and try to either keep this runner on second or get them out at third.

- Use both hands—when you are catching a ball, use both hands at all times. This will help to prevent an error from occurring.

- Throw above the cutoff man—this will help your teammate make the decision on what to do. If it is necessary, they will be able to let your ball through or they can cut it off before throwing to another base.

- Pop fly—when one of these heads your way, make sure that you are running on your toes instead of on your flat feet. This makes sure that you are not bouncing around too much while still being able to keep your eye on the ball.

Right Fielder

- Be alert—if you want to play the game, you have to take it seriously. Always be on your toes, pay attention to the game, and never daydream while the game is going on.

- Center hitter—just because you are the right fielder does not mean you cannot help the other fielders. When a ball is heading to the center, back them up. They might miss and then you will be there to help out. Do the same with the second baseman.

- Charge the ball—this is especially important if you have people on the base. You can charge in after the ball so that the momentum is still there when you throw to your cutoff man.

- Glove is your hand—some people new to the game are not used to the glove and treat it as a foreign object. To be successful in this position, the glove needs to be a part of your hand. This will make it feel more natural to catch the ball.

- Use both hands—this is a good way to catch the ball because it makes sure that you do not lose it from falling out of the glove. The second hand, usually the right, can trap the ball inside the glove.

Pitcher

- Do not become predictable—you want to confuse the other player and make them have no clue what you will do. This will make it more likely that they will miss and strike out.

- Have the inside of the plate become yours. You will then be able to attack from the inside and often the hitter will not be able to handle the fastball that you are throwing.

- Start out the game with some of your stuff that is off speed. This could include the curve or the change up. Save the better stuff for later when the team needs it more. Giving away your good stuff early lets the other team get used to and prepared for it and this can make things more difficult.

- Change the level of your pitches often. For one pitch, make it low while the other pitch can be high. This will confuse them and they will have difficulties guessing where it is going to go next.

- Do a change up whenever it is needed. This will keep the batters on their toes and they will not be able to guess where you are going to throw the ball next.

Catcher

- Keep knees to the middle—this can help you to keep your knees steady. While some catchers will do this in the hopes of blocking others from seeing their signs, this also prevents your own players from seeing the signs.

- Balance on the toes—this can give you a little more balance. If you point the toes to the side a little bit, the squat will feel more comfortable and will keep your knees in the right place. Keep the heels in the air just below the butt.

- Use the mitt—if you want to hide your signs, use the mitt. This can keep the coach on third base from seeing what you are trying to do.

- Keep to the body—always keep the signs as close to the body as possible. This prevents others from seeing and makes it more likely that you and your team will be the only ones to catch the sign.

- Use the fingers—this is the only thing you should be using to make the signs; the rest is just laziness. Exaggerated movements are not needed and are only going to ensure the other side sees them.

Batter

- Adjust to a pitch on the inside—this is the most common of the hitting strategies. Most pitchers are going to try to keep the ball far from you so look out to the outer parts of the plate.

- Aggressive swing—you need to have an aggressive swing ready to go for the best results. If a ball is coming towards you at 90 mph, you need to be able to see the pitch quickly and hit it hard enough to change the direction. Being aggressive helps this to happen.

- Strike zone—if you have a fastball coming your way, attack it in the strike zone. If the ball is not in the strike zone, let it go past and wait for the next.

- Narrow the amount of plate coverage—you will not be able to manage both sides of the plate because it is just too much room. Pick one or more and stick with it because you will have better success.

- Predict the pitch—take a look at the way the pitcher is winding up to try and predict the kind of throw they will be doing. This will get easier as you go along. When you are able to predict, it is easier to determine how you should hit.

Each of the infielders has specific strengths which cause him to be especially good at his position. For example, the first baseman is frequently responsible for forcing outs by stretching his arm out and making catches. Throws to first base are pretty common, so this is a position which always needs to be alert and ready. With second and third base, ground balls are really common so these basemen need be strong fielders. The baseman at third should have a strong arm as that's the longest distance to cover back to home base.

Finally, you have the outfielders. There are three positions in the outfield- the left fielder, center fielder and right fielder. These guys are responsible for catching any fly balls that escape those in the infield. They've also got to be fast on their feet so that they can chase the ground balls that slip past those closer to the batter. All of these positions rely on speed a lot of the time, none more so than the center fielder. The center fielder has the most ground to cover as his territory is the most objective. The right fielder should have a very strong arm. They frequently are responsible for throwing out a runner who is passing third or heading home. A left fielder should be strong defensively. Many hits go out to left field as it's a natural trajectory for a batter swinging strong with his right arm.

There are also less common but still necessary roles on each team. They include the relief pitcher, which enters the game if the starting pitcher shows any signs of injury or fatigue. Another vital role is the closer. The closer is a relief pitcher. In a very close game if your team is winning, you may put in a closer who specializes in getting those clutch end of game outs.

Make sure that you try all positions and see what you're most comfortable with. Ideally, after practice and training you'll be a utility player. A utility player can play multiple positions and move around the field as needed.

Conclusion

I hope that you have enjoyed learning about all the things that you can do to improve your baseball game. Be sure to keep these things in mind:

- Try each baseball position at least once and become a valuable asset to your team by becoming a utility player, someone who can take any role on the team easily. Train for strength, speed, balance and strategy. All are equally important. Great drills to practice are sprints, practicing pitches and catches with a friend or visiting batting cages in your local neighborhood. Baseball requires a strong core, arm and leg muscles so take this into account when hitting the gym. Make sure that you're stretching properly before and after each workout, practice and game so that you don't stretch or tear any muscles.

- Nutrition is paramount for success in a baseball practice or game. This means small healthy meals and snacks throughout the day so that you avoid a spike in blood sugar and lack of energy later on. Focus on carbohydrates that you can burn through easily (complex or fibrous), fruits and veggies and light proteins. Do not eat less than an hour before a practice or game, but do eat immediately after a game. Avoid heavy proteins and fats as they'll put additional stress on your stomach and sit for longer periods of time.

- Hydrate as much as possible. This means water or electrolyte beverages, no dairy, juice, sodas or alcohol. Test how much water you lose in a workout by weighing yourself before and after.

- Figure out your motivation and chase it. You may be a player that dominates with your mind and helping out with strategy. You may be a player that feeds on aggression and needs to hit your hardest and run you're fastest. Remember that you can only succeed as an individual if you succeed as a team. Use your strengths to help out your teammates so that you all win.

- Be sure that you are getting enough rest, that you are visualizing your success at least twice daily, that you are working on keeping a positive mental outlook, that you are making goals and reviewing them daily and that you are working to improve yourself as an individual and a team player each and every day.

Baseball can be a fantastic sport that is so well loved in this country. Following the easy strategies in this guidebook are guaranteed to increase your game and give you an edge above the rest of the competition. Go ahead and take the top five strategies or tips that you think will improve your game the most and relentlessly practice at them until they have been mastered. Then work on your next five strategies. Be persistent, train hard and keep a sharp mental focus so that you can become the hero at your next game!

Finally, if you discovered at least one thing that has helped you or that you think would be beneficial to someone else, be sure to take a few seconds to easily post a quick positive review. As an author, your positive feedback is desperately needed. Your highly valuable five star reviews are like a river of golden joy flowing through a sunny forest of mighty trees and beautiful flowers! *To do your good deed in making the world a better place by helping others with your valuable insight, just leave a nice review.*

My Other Books and Audio Books
www.AcesEbooks.com

Popular Books

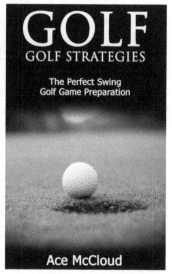

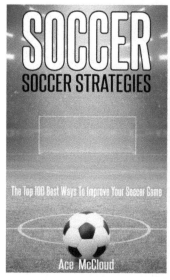

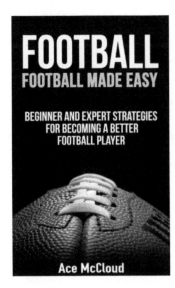

FOOTBALL
FOOTBALL MADE EASY

BEGINNER AND EXPERT STRATEGIES
FOR BECOMING A BETTER
FOOTBALL PLAYER

Ace McCloud

MOTIVATION

MASTER THE POWER OF MOTIVATION
TO PROPEL YOURSELF TO SUCCESS

Ace McCloud

LOSE WEIGHT

THE TOP 100 BEST WAYS
TO LOSE WEIGHT QUICKLY AND HEALTHILY

Ace McCloud

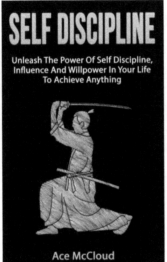

SELF DISCIPLINE

Unleash The Power Of Self Discipline,
Influence And Willpower In Your Life
To Achieve Anything

Ace McCloud

Ace McCloud

HABIT

The Top 100 Best Habits
How To Make A Positive Habit Permanent
And How To Break Bad Habits

ATTITUDE

Discover The True Power Of
A Positive Attitude

Ace McCloud

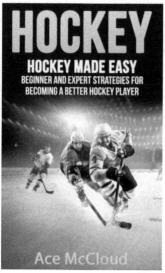

Be sure to check out my audio books as well!

Check out my website at: www.AcesEbooks.com for a complete list of all of my books and high quality audio books. I enjoy bringing you the best knowledge in the world and wish you the best in using this information to make your journey through life better and more enjoyable! **Best of luck to you!**